What Mama Never Told Me about Men, Motherhood, and Marriage

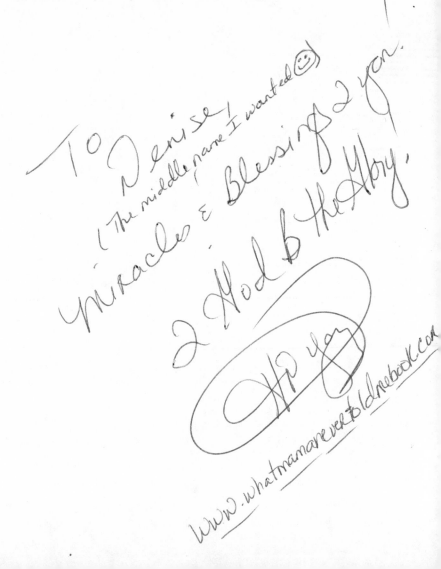

To Denise!
(The middle name I wanted 😊)
Miracles & Blessings 2 you.
2 God b the Glry.
HP you
www.whatmamanevertoldmebook.com

What Mama Never Told Me About Men, Motherhood, and Marriage

The Lessons Learned

Volume 1 of 3: Men

Heather Young
with Tanya Young

To order additional copies of this book, contact:
Xlibris Corporation
1-888-795-4274
www.Xlibris.com
Orders@Xlibris.com
68577

Contents

To the women, daughters, wives, and mothers around the world who have asked themselves, why didn't I know this before I encountered men, motherhood, and marriage?

~

Life is not about waiting for the storm to pass. It's about learning to dance in the rain.

—Anonymous

~

Preface

What my mama never told me is an account of relationship lessons that my sister and I have learned along the way—the hard way. Mama represents anyone who had an influence in raising you—whether this is your biological mother, foster mother, adoptive mother, grandmother, aunt, or a big sister. It may be the case that this information was shared with us, and we didn't listen, didn't understand, or the information was implied. Our mother taught us so much, and she is a great mother whom we love dearly. But no parent is perfect, and no parent can know all, do all, tell all, and be all. That is why no parent would dispute the African proverb that "it takes a village to raise a child." So allow us to be a part of that village and share some of our knowledge, lessons, hurts, and revelations.

Acknowledgments

To my Lord and Savior, through him I move and have my being. I now know and understand your promises are true. Greater is He that is in me than He that is in this world.

To my mother, whose unselfish love, grace, and support continue to strengthen and amaze me. Even though I am writing a book about some of the things she didn't tell me, she showed me so much more. Most of which I could not appreciate until I became older and wiser.

To my father, for his wisdom, wit, discipline, protection, and guidance. Many of my chips fell from his block.

To my twin sister, Tanya, my supreme rock and inspiration. For you know the plans that God has for you. Keep that light shining bright, your whispers were the biggest and loudest. Thank you for believing in me more than I believed in myself. Thank you for loving me for me from birth to salvation.

To my other rocks—Nadine, Cheryl, Cynthia, Wally, Darryl, Eddie, Ben, and Rich. Your love and guidance have been beyond measure.

To Aunt E., a real butterfly with strong wings and endless wisdom.

To Grandma Hylton and Grandma Mae, Pops, Aunt B., Aunt Mercedes, Aunt Eleanor, Aunt Edith, Uncle Mac, Uncle Clifton, and Uncle Edmond, who went before us to establish their place in heaven. Your light shines down from above.

To all the members of the McPherson, Brown, Hylton, Pinto family of which I am so proud to have been grown from. "We are a family in Strength"

To Aunt Margaret, Margaret Ann, Harold and family, your love and support is without measure.

To my nieces LaRissa and Holley, and my great neices, Tianna and Camryn, whom I especially share these lessons with in preparation for their journey into encountering men, motherhood, and marriage.

To my nephews Eddie Jr., Jamal, Ben, Wally III, Joshua, D.C., David, and Daniel, I pray that you become the men God called you to be.

To my prayer warrior and spiritual hero, cousin Cristie White, thank you for praying me out.

To Jules, you are a gem. Thank you for being a real jewel of a friend when I needed you most.

To all of my precious friends, some of whom have also whispered in these pages.

To a small town on Long Island, New York, called Gordon Heights, where villages still raise children.

A special thank-you to Dr. Jamal Harrison Bryant, founder and pastor of Empowerment Temple AME, Bishop Walter Scott Thomas, pastor of New Psalmist Baptist Church, and Dr. Karen Bethea, pastor of Set The Captives Free Outreach Center in Baltimore, Maryland, for their powerful ministries. It is through their teachings, gifts, and visions that Tanya and I have grown spiritually, fell in love with Jesus, and developed an awesome relationship with God.

To my sisters in Christ at First Baptist Church of Glenarden in Glenarden, Maryland. Thank you for your kind words, transparency, and support through our eighteen-month journey to become "Queens of Christ." God used you to help prepare me for "such a time as this." To God be the glory!

Introduction

Family history, heirlooms, superstitions, and wives' tales are often passed down from generation to generation. But have you ever wondered why your mama never told you or waited to tell you about her experiences with men, motherhood, and marriage? Why these life experiences are kept such a mystery until a period of time after you are actually knee-deep into men, motherhood, or marriage? Why mothers, aunts, and grandmothers do not share their stories and lives until it is a day late and a dollar short? When growing up and entering grown-up situations, the questions that need to be asked are not known until we are immersed into the situation. Why aren't women transparent with one another? Do you find yourself saying, "If I only knew before"?

I grew up in a household where children were better seen and not heard. As the youngest, having three elder sisters and an elder brother, I felt like what I had to say wasn't important. I learned early about back talk, so that was another reason to just be quiet. I became a great listener. Our eldest sister and my father would have countless conversations or debates on politics, education, community, celebrities, and whatever they could think of. I listened to the adult conversations around me and processed them with my child's mind. What I thought as a child, I thought was true for an adult. As I became an adult, I realized that what I thought about adults and life as a child was very far from the truth. I felt this was a disadvantage for me because I often learned things the hard way. I remember laughing one day thinking, *I am in my late twenties, and I am supposed to be an adult, but I still feel like a child on the inside.* I thought as a child that when I became an adult, that I would have it altogether, would be confident and never afraid, would be free, and life would be great. I learned that what is seen on the outside can be very different from what people feel on the inside. Youth may look at me thinking that I have it together, I am never afraid, etc., but I am just another female on the journey of what we call life. Whenever I would ask questions, especially to my father, he would say, "What, are you writing a book? Well, leave that chapter out," so now I am writing a book to answer the questions in all those chapters that were left out!

~

Each chapter in this book will highlight a significant challenge when dealing with the male species, and also, a story will unfold right in between. The chapters will also contain biblical scripture references to ponder if you choose to do so. The story entitled "Leah's Heartache" is about the tumultuous yet endearing relationship of a sophisticated young woman named Leah and a captivating young man named Al. But first, let me tell you about the first challenge of dealing with the male species—the BSD factor.

~

What Mama Never Told Me about Men

~

Men-dingo

The BSD Factor

Buy the truth and do not sell it; get wisdom,
discipline and understanding.
—Proverbs 23:23

My mama never told me about the BSD factor; that is, men will

Be anything,
Say anything,
Do anything.

Men will BSD in order to obtain one thing from you and one thing only—*sex*. Yes, I said it; men will *be* anything, *say* anything, or *do* anything to get *sex*. Listen, don't be fooled. I am warning you. Your mama may have told you the old saying "beware of a wolf in sheep's clothing." Well, she was right, and it applies to just about every man I have ever met. I say "just about every man" because there are some good men out there who have matured beyond their flesh and *one* incredible man who I will tell you about later. I have traveled to and from and met men from many places. Time and time again, they prove to be the same. They are hunters by nature, and you are their prey. The good news is just because men think with the wrong head, doesn't mean we as women have to. My mission is to equip you with information that may save you some heartache, time, money, and energy in your relationships with men.

Men Will *Be* Anything

Men are like superheroes, able to self-promote and transform themselves into whatever they want to be. I have met more engineers, entrepreneurs, doctors, lawyers, and the like masked as mailmen, train conductors, and meter men. If men could somehow get away with saying they were the president of the United States, they would.

They Will *Say* Anything

Like superheroes, men can not only leap tall buildings in a single bound, but also stretch the truth for miles. I didn't find out until I was thirty-five that my very own father played a superhero. He told my mother when they were dating that he could not have any kids. Needless to say, I am the last of six children. Do I need to say more?

Ladies, guard you heart! Guarding your heart begins with guarding and arming your mind with knowledge and truth.

The more I read what Mama calls the Good Book, the more understanding I receive about truth. Yes, I am referring to the Holy Bible, one of the greatest stories ever told and our manuscript for living a successful and purposeful life. The following scripture references illustrate God's promise to reveal truth to us when we get to know him:

> Then the woman said to Elijah, "Now I know that you are a man of God and that the word of the Lord from your mouth is the truth." (1 Kings 17:24)

> Guide me in your truth and teach me, for you are God my Savior, and my hope is in you all day long. (Psalms 25:5)

> Do not withhold your mercy from me, O LORD; may your love and your truth always protect me. (Psalms 40:11)

They Will *Do* Anything

I have asked men what was the wildest thing they have ever done or the farthest they have traveled in a single night for *sex*. Well, the shortest distance was their "married with children" next-door neighbor, and the furthest distance was a red-eye flight from the East to West Coast.

From drinks they call Panty Pullers to wining and dining, the result is the same. When a man is on the hunt, he will *be* anything, *say* anything, and *do* anything to accomplish his mission.

The only man in history that did not have to hunt for his woman was Adam. *God* gave *Adam* his helpmate, Eve.

Genesis 2:18, 22, and 23 reads, "The Lord God said, "It is not good that the man should be alone; I will make him a helper suitable for him." Then the Lord God made a woman from the rib he had taken out of the man, and he brought her to the man. The man said, "This is now bone of my bones and flesh of my flesh; she shall be called 'woman' for she was taken out of man."

Men will BSD for sex, but when a man of God is ready to get married, then he will be on the hunt for a wife. At that point, he will be real because he wants a wife who is real. When he finds you, what condition will you be in? Will you be wife material? Someone he can take home to his mama?

Remember, ladies, you are queens of Christ. You should not be doing the hunting; rather, you should be preparing yourselves to be the virtuous woman that God has called you to be. As so eloquently illustrated in the book of Esther, this preparation takes time, obedience, and spiritual wisdom. You are not ready to make plans with another person until you know the plans that your creator has for you. This comes from having a personal and intimate relationship with Christ first! Only then will you be ready to receive the king that God has prepared for you.

Remember, life is a journey with peaks and valley's, but keep your faith for with God and the right knowledge you can make better decisions. Aren't you glad I told you? Now that you know, what will you do differently? After all, this is what this book is about. Don't say I never told you what Mama didn't.

Leah's Heartache

Leah met Al in a nightclub while on vacation. She was visiting a friend, and he happened to be in the area doing the same. Al was very charming and quite handsome, with a body right out of *Muscle Magazine*. To Leah's surprise, as well as delight, she also learned, while on the dance floor jamming to some old-school classics, that Al was endowed with large muscles in every place on his body. Leah and Al danced all night long. If Al had his way, the evening would have ended back in his hotel room, but Leah was not that type of lady. Instead, she accepted his phone number and ended the night with a sincere and gentle hug. Al suggested Leah give him a call the next day for perhaps a day at the beach. There was something about Al that intrigued Leah. Perhaps it was his sunken eyes and that lasting gentle hug before she left the club that night. Perhaps it was that she found it strange that he was the third "engineer" that she had met that night.

Leah called Al the next day. She discovered they had many things in common, and he had a very attractive voice over the phone. As they continued to talk, Leah was shocked to find out that when he referred to himself as an engineer, he was referring to driving a train! (Men will *be* anything.)

Leah and Al did not get a chance to see each other again before leaving that weekend, but Leah had the feeling that this certainly would not be their last encounter.

Leah and Al began communicating over the phone quite frequently. Not more than two days would go by without either Leah or Al calling the other. Leah resided in Chicago while Al lived in St. Louis. The phone calls tended to last for hours. It seemed as though they could talk to each other forever without getting bored or running out of things to say. A real friendship developed where if they did not talk to each other before the day ended, it felt like something was missing. This went on for over three months before Al suggested they meet. They chose a location that would be midpoint between their cities and a place of interest to the both of them. Leah was excited to meet Al, and although they had become good friends over the phone, she feared she would not be able to fight temptation if she stayed in the same room with him. Al suggested double beds rather than separate rooms and told Leah that he would be on his best behavior. They agreed to meet.

It had been so long since Leah had seen Al that she really did not have a good mental image of what he looked liked. After all, they had met in the evening, at a night club. She did not know if she would recognize him in a crowded room or even find him attractive. Leah and Al finally met again, and needless to say, it was what some might call love—or lust—at first sight. The connection that they made over the phone was magnified times ten in person. They had a fabulous evening and retired to their room, which happened to only occupy one bed. According to Al, the hotel was out of double beds. (Men will *say* anything!)

. .

As you read on, remember Leah's story and the BSD factor. Don't let lust blind you. In fact, if you manage to take it out of the equation altogether, you will have twenty-twenty vision.

Men-ded

There is a tie that binds

Though one may be overpowered, two can defend themselves.
A cord of three strands is not quickly broken.
—Ecclesiastes 4:12

My mama never told me about soul ties. She said her mother never talked about it with her, and I guess she subconsciously followed the same. I remember being around twelve or thirteen years old when my mother decided that she needed to talk to my twin sister and me. I could tell that she was nervous and felt awkward about the topic, and at the time, I did not understand why. Since I could tell that she did not want to talk about it, then I did not either. Mama finally got up the nerve to broach the topic and said she wanted to talk to us about the birds and the bees. The birds and the bees? That is not what we expected, and due to our uneasiness of the topic with our *mama*, we told her we already knew. Our mother was kind enough to respond with, "Oh, okay," and never discussed the subject again. That was my way of not having the conversation, and it gave my mother an out as well. However, what she didn't know was that what I knew of "the birds and the bees" was what I heard on the school bus, saw on TV and in movies, and what I read in books.

I was prepared for my menstrual cycle because of how it was explained in Judy Blume's novel *Are You There God? It's Me, Margaret.* When I got my menstrual cycle, I was ready. I called my mother to let her know *not* that I cut myself down there but that I had gotten my period and was on my way to becoming a young woman. When I got my period, I did not know that meant the start of the cycle of life, that technically, I could have a child at thirteen years old if I had sex. It wasn't an issue for me then because sex was the furthest thing from my mind. That was back in the early '80s; oh, how things are different in the twenty-first century. Because my mother and I never had talks about men, I never knew about having a soul tie with a man. I never knew about being heartbroken by someone you loved and who you thought loved you. As I was going through yet another heartbreak and trying to understand what I was feeling, I learned about soul ties.

Soul ties are bonds created when a male and female have sex, when they are united as one as God intended. When parents tell you that you should not have sex, we think they are being strict, old-fashioned, being mean, and don't understand us. They tell us not to have sex because of the fear of getting pregnant, getting an STD—curable and incurable, or getting HIV/AIDS. These are good reasons that males and females should not have unprotected sex. However, there is also another important reason not to have sex, and especially not before marriage. We need to start teaching our children about "soul ties."

A soul tie is the covenant that is made between a man and a woman through sex. A soul tie is a bond that is supposed to last forever. God designed sex for men and women who were married to affirm the ultimate covenant to one another and God. Consequently forever, not just for one night, or for a reason or a season, but for a lifetime. Since the soul tie is not meant to be broken, it is hard to separate yourself from someone that you have had sex with. No matter how bad this man is for you, no matter how much he has hurt you, no matter how much he has taken from you, no matter what he has stolen from you, it is very hard to let go. I never understood why I could not let go. Why I kept giving myself to someone who was so undeserving. Why I could not say no. Why, when I finally said no, it was so easy for that man to turn my no into a yes. It was definitely the soul tie. Save yourself some heartache, wait and take heed. Having sex is bigger than a moment in time, just having some fun for a night, seeking love in the wrong place, or thinking you are grown. You are giving away a part of *you*, your soul—the most sacred and precious part of you. Each time you have sex with a new partner, you continue to give away a piece of you. That decision should not be made haphazardly. Would you give away money or jewelry to someone without trusting that the person would properly care for what you own? When you are no longer with that person, you are left feeling empty and robbed because literally you have been. A piece of you is gone, never to return. Should that person have been given the authority to take from you without expecting to give anything in return? If you value yourself like you should, then you should safeguard your soul from those who do not value the innermost part of you. The right man who God has purposed for you will want you as a person and will wait for *you* and *sex*.

Remember, life is a journey with peaks and valley's, but keep your faith for with God and the right knowledge you can make better decisions. Aren't you glad I told you? Now that you know, what will you do differently? After all, this is what this book is about. Don't say I never told you what Mama didn't.

Leah's Heartache

Leah and Al could not stop seeing each other from that point on. Even though they lived over two hundred miles away from each other, Al managed to come see Leah just about every weekend for almost two years. Time moves quickly when you are in lust. Despite Leah learning that Al was in a relationship, which he indicated was on the rocks, she continued to spend as much time as possible with Al. Leah knew better than to accept or allow this, but somehow got lost in the lust and the time and attention that Al devoted to her. How could he be in a relationship with another woman when he was with her every weekend, on the phone with her every day and several times a day? She had spent weekends at his house. When she saw him and looked into his eyes and had been intimate with him, she felt a soul mate connection that could not possibly be duplicated or shared with anyone else. Leah had tried breaking it off at least a dozen times once she learned he had a so-called girlfriend, but somehow Al knew all the right things to say to make it seem right. Leah could not put all the blame on Al. She had developed deep feelings for him, and she would melt when he was around. Al promised he was not out to hurt her; rather, he was confused and torn between two women he cared for and loved for different reasons. He told Leah that it was rare for him to have a connection like the one he had with her, but he had history with this other woman and felt a sense of loyalty to stay with her. It didn't help that he could do no wrong in this other woman's eyes. That had to be obvious for him to be able to get away with robbing her of any real time spent together. The lies he told must have been enormous for him to be able to pull off a full-time relationship with another woman over two hundred miles away. (I repeat, men will *be*, *say*, and *do* anything.)

To be continued . . .

Men-tion

Standing Ovation

But my mouth would encourage you; comfort from my lips would bring you relief.

—Job 16:5

My mama never told me about sex and its relationship to men. Sex is as important to men as their egos. Just like their egos need stroking pretty frequently, so is their need for affirmation with how they are performing sexually. Just like any other insecurity, men are insecure about sex. No matter how much a man may brag about his sexual confidence, they need to hear that they are pleasing you and continually are desired by you. One of the best things you can do for a man is assure him that he is all that in bed. Even if you both know the sex is good and you have been with a man for a long time, he needs to hear those words of affirmation about what he views as his strongest muscle.

When a man is young, he typically desires quantity. As a man matures and finds out what true love really is, he desires quality. When he finds true love, he may choose to commit and marry. However, despite the rings of commitment, wedding vows, and marriage itself, there is still the risk of his appetite and ego not being satisfied. If you find a good man and want to keep him, make sure that you openly communicate to him how much he satisfies you. Despite what you may think, a man is turned on by knowing that he is pleasing his mate. Even if he doesn't ask how it was, he wants to and is thinking about whether or not he hit the mark. An occasional "thank you" and "honey, you were so good last night" goes a long way.

Also, the more creative you can be in the bedroom, the more pleasing it is to a man. You must be comfortable with your sexuality and be able to talk with your mate about sex. Don't be afraid to tell him what pleases you or ask him what you can do to better please him. Desirability adds to physical attraction. Keep yourself looking good, and reinvent yourself for your mate to keep the desire alive.

Of course, this advice is for when you have been found by your husband. I am not advocating fornication, but many people have sex before marriage, and I am just trying to keep it real for when you have found the real deal.

Eagles, swans, wolves, and Canadian geese are of the few animals in the kingdom that mate monogamously for life. Our odds for monogamy as members of this animal kingdom are not high; however, if you abide with God's plan and purpose for your life, your odds become much greater.

Remember, life is a journey with peaks and valley's, but keep your faith for with God and the right knowledge you can make better decisions. Aren't you glad I told you? Now that you know, what will you do differently? After all, this is what this book is about. Don't say I never told you what Mama didn't.

Leah's Heartache

Leah thought back to her and Al's first encounter. She remembers him calling shortly after he left the hotel. He was obviously dying to know how he had performed the night before. Leah recalls being brutally honest at first and telling him that she felt like he was starring in a movie and that she was his co-star for the evening. Secretly she felt he was so focused on performing his craft while she lay there convicting herself silently for letting things go that far. Leah knew the Holy Spirit was not pleased with her. Even though this man was truly endowed and knew exactly what he was doing, she could not enjoy herself, with thoughts of conviction running through her mind at the time.

Leah could tell by Al's tone that he was disappointed and a little agitated over the phone with Leah's response. Leah wondered, was sex about how the male performed, or how he pleased his woman? He had definitely perfected his craft. *How many women had he been with?*, she thought to herself. Leah remembered the male ego and quickly turned the conversation around by embellishing some of the details of how she felt and playing off her original comments as a way to keep him grounded. Al's tone no sooner changed, and his attention was on hearing more about how he pleased her. Al's famous line became "tell me more about me, baby."

To be continued . . .

Men-age à Trois?

"Down Low" Brothers

Say to the Israelites: "When a man or woman wrongs another
in any way and so is unfaithful to the Lord, that person is guilty."
—Numbers 5:6

My mama never told me about "down low" (DL) brothers. DL brothers are men who have relations with other men. They are often married or have girlfriends but have sex with men on the side. These men do not think of themselves as gay and would be offended if you called them gay. Women are clear on the possibility of a man cheating, but we don't think of him cheating with another man. I could not imagine what it would feel like to have a husband or boyfriend not only cheat, but also cheat with another man. That would be devastating. As women, we try to stay in shape and look good for our men so that they stay attracted to us. Well, how does that come into play when he is cheating with another man? That could really mess up a person's self-esteem.

In my mother's day, if there were "down low" brothers, I don't think it was talked about. There has always been a code particularly in the black community about not spreading family business and keeping secrets. You will hear activists and talk show hosts say today that we have to start talking about our issues in order to change them and begin the healing process.

I am inclined to think that "down low" brothers have always been around but just not talked about. But as we know, everything done in the dark eventually will come to light. The late E. Lynn Harris has been writing about gay relationships for many years, and I read several of his books but never thought about it applying to "my" world. When J. L. King's book was published in 2004, it was big news, and this issue was brought to the forefront. As time passed, it was no longer big news and is not talked about as much. Well, the problem has not gone away, and we cannot forget. I would never want my daughter, niece, mother, cousin, or anyone to get into the predicament of dating or marrying a DL brother and stating that they didn't know. Now that HIV and AIDS have been around for two decades and there are treatments and people are living longer, this disease is not talked about as much either. But it is still a deadly disease that is contracted through blood exchange and sex. We have to always take precautions to protect ourselves. As a friend would always say to me after discussing our crazy experiences with men, "Women have gots to be more careful."

African-American women are still the highest population of new HIV cases. We are still contracting the disease—why? In some cases, it is due to DL brothers. Women have to be conscious of the fact that DL brothers exist. Just because he has muscles, is cool, a professional, works out, and loves sports does not mean he is not on the "down low."

Women need to have open discussions with men about their sexuality. When you are dating someone, the goal is to get data. Some of the questions that should be asked are if the man has ever been with a man, has spent any length of time in jail, when was his last HIV test, and how he feels about gay men or homosexuality. Many women may feel uncomfortable asking these questions. However, how can you feel comfortable giving your precious body to a man but not comfortable to have a discussion with them that can save your life? The majority of men probably will not tell you that they are gay or on the "down low." Often, you can tell by their reaction to the question, their body language, and whether you get a second date. If the man knows you are keying in on these areas and they are on the DL, then they are not likely to pursue a relationship with you. If he lies to you and it comes out later, then you have every right to throw hot grits on him and then beat him with a frying pan. Seriously speaking, it is best to be forewarned and forearmed in any situation.

> I have come as a light to shine in this dark world, so that all who put their trust in me will no longer remain in the darkness. (John 12:46 NLT)

God designed man and woman to be together. The Bible references in Genesis 19 the story of Sodom and Gomorrah where men were wanting to have sex with other men in Lot's house. The behavior of the people angered God, and he destroyed the city by raining down burning sulfur.

Our lives have joy, peace, love, and many blessings when we are obedient to God's commands. It is not always easy because we live in a world of sin, but it is worth every effort to live as sons and daughters of our King.

> Therefore whatever you have spoken in the dark will be heard in the light, and what you have spoken in the ear in inner rooms will be proclaimed on the housetops. (Luke 12:3 NKJV)

Remember, life is a journey with peaks and valley's, but keep your faith for with God and the right knowledge you can make better decisions. Aren't you glad I told you? Now that you know, what will you do differently? After all, this is what this book is about. Don't say I never told you what Mama didn't.

Leah's Heartache

No, Al did not turn out to be a brother on the "down low." Leah did get that right. She asked all the right questions during their initial conversations over the phone. Al most certainly loved woman and woman only.

To be continued . . .

Men-tor

Decisions, Decisions

He who pursues righteousness and love
finds life, prosperity and honor.
—Proverbs 21:21

My mama never told me about dating or courting. Dating is the prerequisite for starting a relationship. Dating should be used for getting data. Once data is received about a person then a decision should be made about the person. The following questions should be asked of yourself—Is this person positive? Is this person someone I should spend time with? Does this person have a relationship with God? Will I be better from having a relationship with this person? Is this person worthy of my time? This thought process allows you to be in control of your life and your future. After answering these questions then an intelligent decision should be made about where this person fits into your life or as we used to say what box am I going to put them in. Some typical boxes are the acquaintance box, the friend box, the boyfriend leading to marriage box, or the trash box.

Often times this is not how dating is performed. Many times a man and woman get together to have dinner and some drinks and if the person is cool and fun then that is the determination of starting a relationship and most times quickly leads into a sexual relationship. What do you really know about the person before giving them your time, your energy, your money, or your self-worth? This is how dating seems to be in the 21st century and it leads to heartache, disease, stalkers, abuse, violence, and sometimes death. There is a better way, a way designed by God and that is courting.

Courting is another way to getting to know someone to make an intelligent decision about them. The difference between courting and dating is that courting is done in a group setting. When courting, the male and female do not put themselves in situations to be alone. Being alone together causes too much temptation to lead to intimacy or build feelings prematurely. When courting, you do not have sex rather you wait until marriage before having sex. While courting, you are in prayer about the relationship and waiting for an answer from God. Courting is introducing the person to parents, family, church family, and friends and doing group activities with people close to you to get to know them and assist you with making an intelligent decision about the person. Whereas in dating by the time the family meets the person, you are already "in love" and do not want to hear anything negative or any constructive criticism about the person. Our family and friends love us and want the best for us and can give an honest opinion about a person. If feelings are not involved it is easier to receive and address any concerns with your family and friends and even with the partner in the courtship. It is not that the family makes the decision for you but they have input and can see things that you may not be able to. They may even ask questions of the person that you may not have thought to ask. After courting for a short period of time (not years) a decision is made as to whether to end the relationship as this person is not who God has intended for you or to continue the relationship and get engaged. Courtships do not normally go on for years because if each of you know that this is who God has ordained for you to marry then there is not a need to wait. Also remember, you are not having sex during the courtship. I ask you to consider courting in your next relationship. Again, courtship is the best way to protect yourself from heartache, disease, stalkers, abuse, violence, and even death at the hands of a loved one.

Remember, life is a journey with peaks and valley's, but keep your faith for with God and the right knowledge you can make better decisions. Aren't you glad I told you? Now that you know, what will you do differently? After all, this is what this book is about. Don't say I never told you what Mama didn't.

Leah's Heartache

Let's just say Leah and Al did not know about courting. Although they did spend several months talking over the phone before they saw each other after meeting at the nightclub, their first meeting immediately changed the future course of their relationship. Leah was away on business. Typically, during these short trips is when Leah was able to reflect and think without the demands of her normally busy schedule. She had the afternoon off after an aggressive morning planning meeting. She decided to get a quick run in before she had to meet up with her colleagues for dinner later that evening. The facility had beautiful walking and running trails on the premises and this afternoon it was 70 degrees and sunny. As she made her way through the courtyard heading to the side exit that started one of the trails she intended to run, she noticed an elderly couple sitting on a bench holding hands and talking as if no one else in the world existed but the two of them. She smiled and said hello as she passed them, but they were so wrapped up in their own conversation, neither likely seen nor heard her as she passed. This is the kind of intimacy she wanted to have with her lifelong mate. She often wondered how couples managed to sustain intimacy like that couple after so many years. With the divorce rate being so high these days, most couples must outgrow it, she thought to herself as she bent over crossing one leg over another for a final stretch before she ran. She remembered the last time her and Al were together, she grinned and smiled as she ran. Now that is intimacy also she thought to herself. She got hot just thinking about it. Focus and reflect Leah, she said to herself. She knew deep down that physical intimacy could not outlast emotional and spiritual intimacy. The physical intimacy she had with Al was like none other she had experienced before. Just last night before she left to go out of town, Al had called her because he knew he would not be able to see her until the following weekend. Their evening chats would start out normal with a recap of each other's day, but before long they would reminisce about the last time they were physically together and how it felt to each other. Before long they would have phone sex and would be able to climax at the same time. Now that is some physical, emotional, and spiritual kind of chemistry, Leah screamed out loud awaking some birds in the trees along the runner's path. How does he do that? is this right? she wondered. He was the only man that could make her have an orgasm over 10 times in one evening, have an orgasm over the phone while being several states apart, AND at the same time too; now that was staying power, she chuckled to herself. She recalled the first time it happened over the phone. She did not believe that he came as she had or finished the same time that she did. Within seconds she got picture mail on her phone which confirmed the fact for her.

Leah reached the half way marker of the 3 mile intermediate challenge trail. She slowed down to adjust her iPod strap which was falling down her arm at this point and to tighten her shoe laces. Half way there Leah said to herself, focus and we can have a scoop of ice cream for dessert later. This was Leah's way of motivating herself during a run. Just do it now and you will be rewarded later, but just in moderation of course. Ok back on the trail Leah began, intimacy, intimacy, intimacy, Leah recanted over and over again. She recalled reading in her favorite monthly magazine that psychologist reported that most couples outgrow physical intimacy within 18 months to 3 years maximum. You know that passionate love that starts off with butterflies in your stomach when you first meet someone. The daydreaming and yearning to touch that person again moments after you have left them. But intimacy that comes with friendship is what really lasts a lifetime. More the reason to get to know a person inside and out as a friend first. She felt like she did that with Al over the phone, but because their relationship was not completely open, she did not bring him around her family nor did she meet his parents or his family to really know his world outside of her and their relationship. Oh, how she wished things could be different between she and Al. Al was in tune with her frequency like no other. He was different. He was sensitive to her needs and feelings not only physically, but emotionally as well. Their soul tie at this point was not only physical but emotional also. She could not let that go. She could not reverse or slow down the pace at which her feelings and desires ran for him. She wished things had started out different between them. Perhaps she should have agreed to meet him for a matinee movie or lunch with a group of friends.

To be continued . . .

Men-opause

Little Boys
Having Manly Experiences

When I was a child, I talked like a child, I thought
like a child, I reasoned like a child. When I became
a man, I put childish ways behind me.
—1 Corinthians 13:11

My mama never told me how important it is to digest information pertaining to a man's childhood experiences. If you don't remember anything else, please remember this: a man's childhood accounts for 90 percent of who he was yesterday, who he is today, and who he will be tomorrow. Many men are walking around with mommy and daddy pains from adolescence and childhood, but are too prideful to realize or deal with those internal pains. The statistics of the number of men and women who have grown up with an absentee mother or father, either physically or emotionally, is alarming. Those that were fortunate enough to have both parents also may have unresolved trauma in their lives that has not been dealt with. No matter how good they may appear on the outside, some damage has been done and may not match how they feel or look on the inside. There is always a cause and effect. Like Newton's law states, "For every action there is an equal and opposite reaction." If there was trauma or drama left untreated, then there is physical and/or emotional damage to the being. You must uncover to what extent and how it may impact your relationship or the relationship with your future children. I don't know why, but we seem to be so naive to this. Just like you know your best friend and why she is the way she is, you need to know your man in that same manner. Most men don't believe in counseling. They are so prideful that they cannot imagine needing anyone to help them. In order for them to go to counseling, they would have to admit there is a problem. If they admit there is a problem, then they would have to go a step further and fix the problem.

Think about the African American race and its times of enslavement. Would you consider slavery a traumatic experience? Think about being traumatized and never having been given therapy or counseling for that trauma. Consider a deep laceration or broken bone that receives no medical attention. You can continue to function; however, there would be scar tissue and a bone out of place—never mended. Sure you can function, but you would likely be functioning with some sort of defect or deficiency. It may be hidden but, at some point, will be revealed. If an open sore is left untreated, there is also the risk for further damage. When the untreated open wound is exposed to other external elements such as bacteria, the wound can become infected and lead to a more serious condition than initially started. An infection left untreated could bring on a fever. Furthermore, a fever untreated could lead to detrimental ailments, organ failure, and so on until, ultimately, death.

Now in comparison, take a man enslaved; one day he is set free. Set free with no therapy. His first instinct is survival. He must forge ahead and try to survive and provide for himself, which does not leave any time for help or treatment. He must educate himself and work to sustain himself. Now make his working conditions difficult and throw in unfair treatment without recourse for this free man. On top of the current conditions, this man still has the hurt and pains of slave masters sleeping with his woman and female family members, mistreating his children, and the threat of killing him if he gets out of line. After over four hundred years of slavery, this is generational years of abuse and trauma left untreated. Now these free men have children of their own and pass down untreated side effects of this drama and trauma. It may become a little less noticeable generation after generation as progress has been made, but it is still there. I digress that far back in time to give you an illustration of what I mean by having a traumatic event take place as a child and never getting the appropriate treatment to heal from it. Our men go from boys to men, but their minds are still caught in the childhood experiences. These childhood experiences could involve sexual molestation, physical abuse, and/or rejection from a parent. This is what I mean when I say they are little boys having a manly experience.

In the case of trauma from a sexual encounter, boys will never tell if they were seduced by an older woman into having sex. Despite perhaps feeling violated, in their mind they are a man and are supposed to want sex. Most men that I have met had their first encounter with an older woman that took advantage of them and their boyhood. Given the same circumstances with a young female and an adult male, this would be considered rape. When a little boy is sent off to camp, many parents do not think about the possibility of their little boy being molested. A man's first encounter in a female relationship plays a huge role in how they may view women and their own sexuality.

When dealing with a man who is dealing with issues from childhood, you may need to return to that little boy to discover the real issues that are manifesting in adulthood. You may be dealing with an issue today with your man that has nothing to do with today at all. You may have to find the root of the problem in his roots. Then once discovered, approach it as if you were dealing with a child, because in his mind, the problem is still there as if he is still a child.

It will take the grace of God to overcome, but there is victory in believing, trusting, and casting your cares upon the Lord.

Remember, life is a journey with peaks and valley's, but keep your faith for with God and the right knowledge you can make better decisions. Aren't you glad I told you? Now that you know, what will you do differently? After all, this is what this book is about. Don't say I never told you what Mama didn't.

Leah's Heartache

Leah rolled over and caught a glimpse of the sun peeking through the curtain that was partially closed in the penthouse suite where she and Al had spent the evening. She was deep in thought when Al pulled her closer to him and held her tight. This hug felt different. She turned to face him and gave him a kiss on his forehead. Al cracked a smile as he stretched his arms around her again. Leah felt a teardrop on her forearm. "Baby, what's wrong?" she asked. Al confidently replied, "Nothing," as he rubbed his eyes and mumbled, "I have allergies."

After some stroking and setting the right atmosphere, Al finally did open up and share the cause of the teardrop. Because of Al's experience of being molested by an older woman at the age of eleven, he never had the chance to determine his own view and type of relationships he would have with women. This first encounter made him feel more like an object that was being used versus a sincere display of affection. Subconsciously, he adopted the philosophy of "hit it and split it." He never really allowed himself to completely open up and truly love a woman. Leah was able to touch places in Al that he himself did not want to go. At this moment with Leah, he felt true love, and it felt good. He had never shared this childhood experience with anyone before. This is the relationship and love he had been searching for. But it hurt him because he felt he could not make things right. He thought of all the women he had hurt in the past. He kept saying he could not make it right. Leah told him he could, but he kept saying he could not, and she did not understand what he meant and why until . . .

To be continued . . .

Men-ace

The Master's Touch

"Love the Lord your God with all your heart and
with all your soul and with all your mind.
—Matthew 22:37

My mama never told me about abuse. Did she think she needed to? Probably not. She raised a strong, intelligent, independent woman. She always told me to take care of myself and not to depend on anyone else. I looked healthy, I laughed and smiled a lot, and she saw a normal young woman. The world saw a normal young woman with a bright future. What people see on the outside is not always what we feel or know to be on the inside. I say "know to be on the inside" because of what goes on in our minds. I would tell anyone that no man would abuse me. I would tell myself that I would never let a man abuse me. In my mind, abuse was a man giving you a black eye or throwing you down a flight of stairs, leaving bruises on you, or putting you in the hospital. That is what abuse was to me, and I would never let it happen to me. Well, those things never did happen to me, but I was abused in my relationships. I was abused verbally, physically, and mentally. When I began to grow in Christ was when I began to realize that I was a child of God. A child of God is to be treated royally as heirs of the kingdom. The children of God have a treasure inside of them that is precious. I began to get to know God and search after the things of God. As I grew in Christ, I began to realize that what I thought was normal in a relationship was not normal, but rather was abuse. Even though I did not grow up in an abusive household, the things that I saw around me and what I took in over the years made me believe that arguing and fighting in a relationship were normal. Everyone argued and fought every now and then. It just happened, and my relationships were not any different. I grew up in a household where if you did something wrong, you were punished. There was some type of consequence for bad behavior or for not following the rules. This mentality carried over into my relationships. When I did something that my mate didn't like and he yelled at me or shoved me or called me names, it was a consequence to my "bad" behavior or the spoken or unspoken rule that I did not follow. When people get upset, they curse, they call you names, they may put their hands on you. Isn't this normal? No, it truly is not. You may wonder how women end up in abusive relationships. It may be because of an abusive parent or family member. It may be due to the violence they experience in their community. It may be from low self-esteem brought on by their peers. It may be because of life experiences that caused them to stop loving themselves. Somehow, abuse became normal to them. Because I fought back, I thought it was not abuse. It didn't dawn on me that we should not be fighting in the first place, that human beings are not meant to hurt each other and are meant to only love each other.

> Dear friends, let us love one another, for love comes from God. Everyone who loves has been born of God and knows God. Whoever does not love does not know God, because God is love.
>
> (1 John 4:7-8)

The beginnings of relationships are fun and exciting, and I was always treated the way that I want to be treated—which is why I continued dating the person. Everything is good, and then I noticed that over time, the relationships would slowly deteriorate. A light would go on that there wasn't as much fun or there weren't as many good times. When I questioned this, I was told by one mate that that was the honeymoon stage and that the honeymoon stage was over and the relationship wasn't supposed to be like that anymore. Well, I wanted to continue in the honeymoon stage and spent many years trying to get back there, and I never did. Oftentimes, people put their best self forward and say and do all of the things that the other person wants to hear. Remember the BSD factor I told you about in the first chapter. They do the things to get the person. Some may call it the chase or the conquest. Once the conquest is won and if it's just a conquest, then the thrill goes away, and the relationship is no longer what it used to be. Well, by that point, I was in love and did not want to let the relationship go. It hurt too much to let go. So I would wait and wait for it to get back to being "good." I learned that in a healthy relationship, both parties must have a desire to finish as they started. The finish may be until death do us part, but whenever and however the relationship ends, it should not be because the person is no longer who you thought they were. Someone always ends up hurt when a relationship is not based on truth. If you don't like to cook, don't cook to get the man and then stop once you are committed or married. Be honest; if you don't like to cook, then say that you don't like to cook, because that is who you are. You want your mate to accept you for who you are. If you don't have extra cash to purchase lavish gifts and expensive dinners, then don't do those things to get the person. It is great to want to do something nice for someone and take them somewhere special, but take them where and when you can. It is awful to enjoy those things with your mate, and then when you are committed, you find out that all of those dinners, lavish gifts, trips, etc., were purchased on credit and your mate is deep in debt. Or your mate did not pay his bills trying to impress you, which led him on the path to bad credit. If you love yourself as Christ loves you, then your dating experiences will not be consumed with those superficial, unproductive stunts. Healthy relationships consist of truth, communication, care, integrity, patience, and eventually, love.

I learned the hard way that a push, a shove, name-calling, yelling, jealousies, and overprotection are forms of abuse. These things should not be a part of your relationship. Wrestling and play fighting are ways of opening the door to abuse. If you can play with each other by hitting each other, wrestling with each other, calling each other hurtful names, then what is to stop you when you are angry at the person? It is best to not introduce this type of entertainment into your relationship. There are other ways to have fun with each other that won't contaminate your relationship.

As I learned these things and began to apply them with the help of God, I began to handle my relationships differently. I began to set the standard on how we would interact and what was expected in the relationship. My mate had to accept the standard that I set, and I would not compromise what I knew was right. I would no longer give in for the sake of having someone, for a good time, or to feel loved. I fell in love with Jesus, and I loved myself, so I didn't need to compromise who I was to be in a relationship. Once I made the appropriate changes, then I began to have healthy relationships; and if the relationship did not last, then it was okay because I knew I either deserved better or that was not the person that God had chosen for me. I only wanted the man that God had for me, and if God closed the door, then I knew that there was an open window somewhere. Once you know better, then you have to do better, get better, and live better.

> This is how we know who the children of God are and who the children of the devil are: Anyone who does not do what is right is not a child of God; nor is anyone who does not love his brother.
>
> (Joshua 3:10)

Remember, life is a journey with peaks and valley's, but keep your faith for with God and the right knowledge you can make better decisions. Aren't you glad I told you? Now that you know, what will you do differently? After all, this is what this book is about. Don't say I never told you what Mama didn't.

Leah's Heartache

Al told Leah for the first time how much he loved her while they lay in that intimate moment of truth. He shared how special she was to him, how she deserved everything that was good in life, and how perfect she was and how effortless it was to love her. Leah was on a constant emotional roller coaster. She felt the same way about Al, but his tie to this other woman constantly haunted her. Al would often need to sneak away to return a phone call privately, and Leah knew exactly whom he had to call. This would hit her like a ton of bricks, awakening her out of the fantasy that she was his only one. Her conscience would eat at her, and humiliation would once again set in.

Leah was a very attractive and confident woman. She never lacked for male attention whenever she would go out. Because she was so caught up with Al, she did not allow herself to be open to advancements from other men. Besides, she spent most of her weekends with Al, not allowing much other time to meet other people. Leah began to feel insecure with herself. She never had a problem with a man choosing her, but somehow this woman stayed above her. Even though the other woman did not have Al's time and attention, she had a commitment when it counted.

Al continued to hide behind his wall of confusion. Leah knew who the author of confusion was and always encouraged Al to return to church and seek spiritual guidance. Al was so genuine when he spoke of being confused, and Leah, on some levels, could identify with Al in not understanding what true love was and why feelings could be had for more than one person at the same time. Leah herself began to believe that love was not a choice, rather commitment to love was.

To be continued . . .

Men-tality

Discovering a Man's Temperament

*So Gideon took the men down to the water. There the LORD
told him, "Separate those who lap the water with their
tongues like a dog from those who kneel down to drink."*

—Judges 7:5

My mama never told me about the different temperaments of men. I
grew up with a love for animals, dogs in particular. When I was younger,
whenever I would see a stray dog in the road, I would ask my mother if
we could pick it up and take it home with us. She would always reply,
"We don't know where that dog has been or what he has, we just can't
bring him home with us." I was always a sucker for a helpless puppy
dog face. It wasn't until I grew older that I began to understand about
the different breeds and subsequent temperaments of dogs; that is, their
innate characteristics. I understood that before you made one a part of
your family, you needed to understand the breed.

Our family dogs were typically German shepherds. This was my father's
breed of choice. I believe this was due in part to his law enforcement
background. German shepherds were police dogs and had certain
characteristics that made them preferred in the law enforcement field.
German shepherds are confident and strong in their behavior as well as
in their appearance. They are not only typically fearless, but they are also
fiercely loyal and protective. They are extremely eager to please and will
fight to the death for the life of their owner. They can appear somewhat aloof,
particularly with strangers, and they take time to get to know new people

before they let their guard down. German shepherds are incredibly alert and never miss anything that goes on around them, which is one of the reasons this breed makes the perfect watchdog. I not only loved large dogs like the German shepherd and rottweiler, but also had an affection for small toy dogs. I knew when I owned a dog as an adult that I would want a small dog in the house. Today, I am the proud owner of a bichon frise named Braxton, and boy, has he taught me a thing or two about himself, myself, and life itself.

I had never even heard of the bichon breed until one day when he was sitting in a cage in my living room as a surprise Valentine's Day gift. The most adorable puppy dog face you could imagine was staring at me with both curiosity and fear. I was happy to learn that he was smart, easy to train, hypoallergenic, did not shed, and would not grow to be more than twenty pounds and twelve inches high. This was my kind of house dog. I named him Braxton after an uppity comedian on a prime-time TV show. He was a silly dog that loved to play, and he needed a distinguished name after learning about his royal and prestigious bloodline. A book about the bichon frise gave me a full history of the breed and explained his temperament. Training him and getting him to do what I wanted as his owner was fairly easy on some fronts, but there were some characteristics that he would never outgrow or change. He had innate characteristics that no matter how hard I tried to change would remain constant.

Bichons are attention seekers as in the life of the party. Whenever I have company over to my house, it is Braxton's opportunity to entertain. Even friends that dislike dogs somehow become Braxton's best friends. He has a propensity to run toward people despite my attempts to call him away or make him sit and stay. When people are around, he has a selective memory regarding the obedience commands he knows all too well. Bichons are also known to have a mind of their own, to be independent thinkers; they get their feeling hurt easily and are extremely loveable. They not only love their owners affectionately, but will also stray away with others if given attention. One time in particular, I dropped him off before work at a local pet store to be groomed. After work, I went to pick him up. The groomers gave me a dog that looked like my Braxton, but something about the dog was different. I stood in the pet store in front of the groomer not only a little puzzled, but also ashamed to not be sure whether this was my dog. The dog was jumping all over me and happy to see me, which even surprised the groomer when I asked him if he was sure this was my dog. He replied, "He seems to have missed you." After carefully looking at the dog, I noticed his teeth were stark white, more like a puppy than my seven-year-old Braxton's teeth. After the groomer did some checking, he indicated they indeed had another bichon in for grooming that day and would call the owner to see if there had been some kind of mistake. Lo and behold, the other owner had not really paid attention and took my dog home with her. She only had her dog for about six months, and though she thought something was different, she had not suspected the pet store would have made such a terrible mistake. Typical of their breed, both dogs would have happily gone home with another owner.

I have had Braxton for over twelve years now, and there are still some things that will just never change about him. These are some of the same things that make him who he is and what I simply love about him. He will always love other people, he will always crave attention, he will always be happy-go-lucky despite old age setting in, and he will probably never sit and stay for long around company. Nevertheless, I would not trade him for the world. As much as I wanted him to sit still and stop craving attention from other people, I never wanted to crush his spirit or change who he was born to be. If I wanted a serene dog, then it would be my responsibility to purchase a bulldog, which is more quiet and lazy. I am almost ashamed to draw the parallel line here, but the same goes for a man.

You must let him be who he is. You really don't have a choice. No matter how much you nag, try to change him, or think he will be different with you, a man, or any person for that matter, is going to revert back to being what is at the core of who they are. What you can do is decide whether he is what you are looking for in a man or whether you can live with the consequences of certain characteristics of him. If he was a cheater when you met him or he cheated on another girl to be with you, more than likely, he will cheat again. If he lies to other people, eventually he will lie to you. If he takes advantage of or abuses other people, eventually he will do the same to you. Now I am not saying that people cannot change, but people have to want to change. Typically, the only time people change is as a result of some traumatic event or an encounter with God. Do your homework and observe and discover his temperaments. In the end, it's all about choices. As you get older and wiser, draw closer to Him that created you and learn from each lesson that He teaches you. Only then will you begin to make better choices.

While we are on the subject of temperament and mentality, I also have a special message for women pertaining to their role in shaping a man's Men-tality. That is; Mama never told me not to play games in my relationships. I learned that men value themselves in a way that many women often do not. Men protect their hearts and emotions much more than woman do. Women love freely and intensely in relationships and at the same time we hurt just as freely and intensely if the relationship fails.

If a man gives of himself freely it is a major privilege for the woman he has chosen to open up to and let into the most precious inner parts of himself. I noticed this when my nephew was a little boy. At the age of 4 he was a loverboy and had a girlfriend in pre-school. I could see the excitement in his eyes of how he liked his 4 year old playmate. He was not ashamed to share the news with his family of his little "girlfriend". He was very sweet and treated his "girlfriend" so nice. It was a picture of "love" at its purest form. Somewhere along the way my nephew was hurt in a relationship or what he thought was a relationship and he no longer displays that zeal in relationships. He no longer freely opens up his heart to the women in his life. Men love just as deeply as women but guard themselves after the first time they become heart broken in a relationship. It could be said that men get hurt in relationships from the women in their lives "playing games". As you read this, you may ask what do you mean playing games? I would go out on a limb and say that all women do it – subconsciously or consciously. Playing games is when we are not honest with the men in our lives about what we want and how we truly feel. This is a self defense mechanism that we as women have learned along the way. We think we are protecting ourselves by not showing the man how much we care, or not speaking up about what we want or feel.

We tell our girlfriends what we want and how we feel but never tell the man we are having the relationship with. By not being honest or upfront with a man then the man is left to assume what you feel, think, need or want. Then we get upset when he doesn't give us what we want or make us feel the way we want to feel. I know men are very intelligent but they are not mind readers. It is our responsibility as women to openly communicate with our mates in a clear manner so that no one has to assume and each person will be clear on what the other wants and needs.

If you are not sure if you play games to protect yourself then ask yourself if you have done any of the things below:

- Ordered a salad on the first date when you are really hungry. If you are hungry then eat! You are playing a game to eat a salad when you would eat a 3 course steak dinner with your girlfriend. I am not saying order the most expensive meal on the menu but be real and eat as you normally would.

- Not saying anything about your upcoming birthday or a special date shared between the two of you in order to find out if he would remember. Doing this is setting your mate up for failure. Does it really mean that your mate does not love you because he did not remember your birthday? It may just be he has a very poor memory. Either way by not saying anything you are not getting your desired result.

- Not taking a man's phone call. We think by not taking a man's phone call we are making them suffer and showing them that we are okay without them. That is not the case when you are sitting home wishing he would call. When you see his number then you get that little smile as though he wants me but decide not to answer the call. Well he did want you but you didn't answer the phone. Not answering the phone purposely is an immature response in a relationship. If you do not want to speak to the person then answer the phone and tell them that you do not want to speak to them and why you do not want to speak to them in a mature manner. Be honest and tell them that you are hurt, confused, need time to think your own thoughts, need some space, etc. By not answering the phone especially nowadays when most people do not leave the house without their phone and are rarely too busy to answer their phone, leads a man to think that you don't care, that you are seeing someone else or that you are . . . playing games.

- That leads me to another way we play games. The classic get back strategy is to make a man think that we are seeing someone else. This is the worst thing that you can do if you want to stay in your relationship and keep your partner's trust. The quickest way to end a relationship or for a man to lose respect for a woman is by having him think you have been with another man (in any manner). As women it is in our nature to forgive and take a man back after he has cheated. I have heard many women say what they would do if they caught their boyfriend or husband cheating but you never know what you would do until you are in that situation. However, if a man says that the relationship is over if he finds out that you cheat then by golly that is exactly what will happen – your relationship will be over! If you have been intimate with another man, show interest in another man, spend time talking to another man then your mate no longer feels special and you are no longer special to him. He no longer feels he is your protector. You have shared yourself with someone else and have become "damaged goods". You have taken away his role in the relationship and given it to someone else.

I have ruined several relationships by playing these games. I am thankful that I dated a man who could explain these things in a way that I could truly understand. The light bulb went on as to what I was really doing. The messages that I thought I was sending was not the message that was being received and I was not getting the result that I wanted—which was keeping my mate. As I began to recognize my childish game playing ways and made the necessary changes is when I began to have healthy, positive, fulfilling relationships. Have you ever noticed that the problem is not getting a man, the problem is keeping the man. I was in sales once and their motto was "The power to close". A good salesperson is one that not only makes the contacts but one who can make the sale – having the power to close. If you desire to be married, stop playing games in your relationship. Be open, honest, and communicate clearly. When the man asks for your hand in marriage then you know . . . you have the power to close!

Remember, life is a journey with peaks and valley's, but keep your faith for with God and the right knowledge you can make better decisions. Aren't you glad I told you? Now that you know, what will you do differently? After all, this is what this book is about. Don't say I never told you what Mama didn't.

Leah's Heartache

Al had two sides to him; one that was charismatic, enterprising, and craved for attention and another that was as innocent as a child that just wanted to be covered and held. He would peel as some men call it, taking off his shirt to show off his six pack abs. Al was into fitness just as much as Leah. She loved the way his body looked just as much as he did and when their bodies connected, there was a flame ignited that took hours to put out. They decided to take a short vacation together after a long winter that never seemed to end that year. Leah had recently returned from a long weekend with her family for Easter and couldn't wait to see Al again.

Leah also felt that this would be just the thing to seal the deal in their relationship. Al would surely break all ties with his so called girlfriend after a vacation with the one he really loved, she thought. Leah stopped by the bank on her lunch break to take out some extra funds for her mini-vacation with Al. As she was leaving the bank and distracted by a crying baby and her mother trying to settle her down in the corner of the bank, she walked straight into a strong figure that nearly knocked her to the ground on impact. Excuse me miss, the gentleman tried to warn just before impact. Leah embarrassed to look up, finally did only to be surprised by a tall handsome man with a friendly smirk on his face. "Are you ok," he said attempting not to laugh in her presence. "Oh Yes," she replied trying to play it cool although her forearm still stung a little from hitting the books he was carrying." I am so sorry, "I wasn't paying attention to what was right in front of me." Leah said. "That's ok, it is not everyday that I get tackled by a woman as beautiful as yourself," he replied." Leah could not help but blush a little as she stared at this gentlemen's warm smile and straight pearly white teeth. She was almost lost for words when her cell phone rang in her purse and she was forced to politely say thank you and excuse me a minute. She dug for her phone that had slid to the bottom of her purse. As she looked at the caller id she noticed the man move towards the bank counter. It was Al calling. To her own surprise she decided not to answer it right then and instead stepped to the side of the counter to reorganize everything that had shifted in her purse, along with her skirt, when she collided with this mystery man. She had many men call her beautiful before, but there was something about the way this particular man spoke that made her believe him. Besides, she and Al had somewhat of an argument earlier over none other than his inability to profess his love for her and only her. Leah decided to give Al a little dose of his own medicine. Just how easy would it be for him if he felt that I had feelings for someone else. No longer would Leah answer his calls on the first ring or be available whenever he called. Leah knew she could love no one other than Al, but wanted to feel like she had some sort of control in their relationship. She had ignored compliments and advancement from other man since she began seeing Al; just maybe it was time to at least hear out another man. She purposely took her time at the counter just in case the man who had just called her beautiful wanted to pay her another compliment. As he completed his transaction at the counter she noticed him look her way. She began to gather her things as he began to walk in her direction. "I am all eyes forward this time," Leah said with a smile, as the man approached her. "Good for you, I hope I didn't do any bodily harm earlier," the mystery man replied. "Nothing a little ice won't cure," Leah replied. "Oh my goodness, so I really did hurt you," the man replied. "No, I am fine really, I am just kidding with you," Leah said. "Well, how about I check on you in a few days to make sure you are OK and perhaps take you to lunch to make up for it?" he asked. "I am sure I am fine really," Leah said as she looked away slowly. "Well at least think about it please," the man said as he reached for his business card.

"Here, take my card, my name is Collins, Ray Collins and you are?" he said. She smiled, "Oh forgive me, Leah, Leah Reynolds." "Well Ms. Reynolds, I hope to hear from you soon," she replied. "Thank you Mr. Collins, very nice to meet you," Leah smiled, as she exited the bank after he politely opened the door for her to leave. As Leah walked to her car and Ray walked to his, Ray shouted across the parking lot, I really hope to hear from you soon Ms. Reynolds. Be safe! Leah turned and smiled with a short wave. Just maybe, Leah mumbled under her breath as she put his card in her coat pocket and got in her car to return to work. Interesting man, she thought just as her cell phone rang. It was Al calling again so she decided to answer. "Hi baby", Leah said. "Don't Hi baby me, I called you three times, why didn't you answer your phone earlier?" Al said. "I, I was tied up at the bank baby, I am sorry I couldn't get to the phone earlier," Leah recanted. "I didn't know you called me more than once," Leah sort of stuttered, although she was telling the truth. "What's up, is everything ok?" Leah firmly spoke.

Al responded, "Well, I didn't like the way we ended our last conversation and I just wanted to let you know that I understand how you must feel baby and I am sorry." "You know I love you baby, Al spoke softly, when we go away tomorrow, I don't want us to be upset about anything. I want to enjoy every minute that I get to spend with my baby." "I love you too baby," Leah responded. "Now let me get back to my lunch date; I mean work," she chuckled. "Don't play with me woman, I couldn't even imagine you with another man," Al said firmly "You are mine and all mine." I know, I know, and I wish I could say the same Leah thought to herself. "Ok, I have to go, but enjoy your day baby, whatever that might consist of," Al concluded as he did most conversations. "Ok, same to you," Leah replied. Leah knew that she had no intentions on calling Mr. Ray Collins and hadn't even looked at his card before she put it away, but she sort of liked the idea of possibly making Al jealous a little to perhaps persuade him to commit to her fully for fear that perhaps someone else would choose her. Mr. Collins on the surface was her type if she ever admitted that she actually had a type of man. Leah was a free spirit. Although she had her standards, she typically was open minded when it came to men. She didn't look to class or status, or the type of shoes a man wore like some of her friends. As long as the man was not out right ugly, she went for the heart and personality. She loved a man that was fairly confident, and sure of himself and was partial to those that could get and keep her attention. Leah did however, prefer men taller than her and with at least a fair build, clean cut, but with an edge. Anyway, what was she thinking—she loved and wanted only to be with Al. She would not do anything to jeopardize her chance to have the most incredible man in the world. She and Al went on their mini-vacation and the long weekend could not have been better for the both of them. Leah was so at peace when they were together and Al had a peace within him that comforted her. He often told her he felt like he could be completely himself around her and she made him genuinely happy. He loved the way they got along and shared the same interests. They both enjoyed fitness, healthy eating, and was adventurous. Their time spent together was what Al termed, "effortless love". Each encounter was filled with excitement and anticipation for both of them. As soon as they saw each other, it was like they had met for the very first time. It was magic and despite their distance, they could easily pick right back up where they left off the last time they saw or spoke to each other. They could spot each other across a crowded room and would be drawn to each other like a magnet. They would be meeting outside of Miami for a little fun in the sun. They both also enjoyed gambling and there were a couple of casinos near Fort Lauderdale that they would go to. Leah loved poker while Al preferred Roulette. They both were risk takers at heart.

Life is a gamble, but only those that played had a chance at winning, Al would often say. I will always bet on loving you Leah, Al called out as he spotted Leah entering the baggage claim area.

Leah turned around and ran to meet Al. Al picked her up and spun her around as he kissed her forehead and then met her lips as they embraced in front of baggage claim number 3. "I missed you," Leah proclaimed. "I missed you more," replied Al. Well you can show me just how much later, Leah whispered, right now I think I see my bag on the carousel. Leah and Al retrieved their luggage, but didn't let go of each other as they hailed a cab to their hotel. They didn't see much of the sun or the casino for the first 24 hours.

Leah rolled over to look at the clock, it was just after 5:00pm and she needed to begin to get ready for dinner. She thought she would just lie down for a minute and rest her eyes as she felt a headache coming on. Neither one of them had gotten much sleep in the past few days for fear they would miss precious moments with each other. She didn't realize that she had slept for just over an hour. This was their last evening together and Al had made them a 6:30 pm dinner reservation. He also had a surprise for her that he had done a good job of keeping a secret the whole weekend. Al must have gone out while Leah took a nap as there was no answer when she called for him. Al should be back any minute now, she thought to herself and perhaps they could be intimate one more time before dinner. All it took was one suggestive look and they might just miss dinner. She heard the doorknob to their hotel room begin to turn, it must be Al returning to their room, she thought to herself, at the same time her cell phone began to ring.

To be continued . . . . .

Men and Love

What's love got to do with it?

*Leah became pregnant and gave birth to a son. She named
him Reuben, for she said, "It is because the Lord has seen
my misery. Surely my husband will love me now."*
—Genesis 29:32

My mama never told me about when a man utters the three little words
"I love you." Just because you hear those magical words from a man, don't
go rushing to the bridal shop to pick out your wedding gown. "I love you"
from a man can have many different meanings and will be said for many
different reasons. Okay, so he said it: "I love you." What does this really
mean in the grand scheme of things? We have all heard it before, and
oftentimes we come to our own conclusions of what it means. It can have
many different meanings from man, but what is truly important is what
God says it means.

> The Bible tells us in 1 Corinthians 13:04-08 (NKJV) that "love
> suffers long and is kind; love does not envy; love does not parade
> itself, is not puffed up; does not behave rudely, does not seek its
> own, is not provoked, thinks no evil; does not rejoice in iniquity,
> but rejoices in the truth; bears all things, hopes all things, endures
> all things. Love never fails."

The Bible teaches that there are four types of love:

- Instinctual—as a mother to her child
- Erotic—as a man to his wife
- Filial—brotherly or sisterly love, love for mankind
- Agape—godly, unconditional love

Agape love, which is the last type of love the Bible speaks of, is the highest love of all. It does not come with terms, conditions, or a trail of other women. It does not hit or abuse emotionally or physically. It thinks no evil. Real love that makes for long-term, positive, and healthy relationships is built on agape love.

You will so call 'fall in love' with many different men throughout your life. We meet people for different reasons, seasons, or a lifetime. The question becomes, which is it? At times, we are with a man with whom we ought to only be with for just a reason or a season. When you first meet, it often seems like he is the one God sent straight out of heaven. Later to discover he was not working with God at all. He was demonstrating the BSD factor to get what he wanted from you. He was not what or who you thought he was at all. Only time and distance reveal this. Time and distance will tell you if a man is truly what he presents at first. A famous comedian said it best, "When you first meet someone, you do not meet them; rather, you are meeting their personal representative." It's not until the third or fourth date or longer that you really meet the person. When you are emotionally involved, it is difficult to see what others clearly see. Although signs and symptoms are there, we often overlook or ignore them. Don't ever ignore your inner voice, for it is your angel speaking to you and trying to protect you from the seen and unseen. Your inner voice is your best counselor because truth is always revealed. Listen and take heed.

Remember, life is a journey with peaks and valley's, but keep your faith for with God and the right knowledge you can make better decisions. Aren't you glad I told you? Now that you know, what will you do differently? After all, this is what this book is about. Don't say I never told you what Mama didn't.

Leah's Heartache

Leah was devastated when she answered her cell phone and heard the voice of the other woman. It was Al's girlfriend—better yet, fiancée, as she referred to herself. She wanted to know why Leah was blowing up her man's cell phone and whether he was with Leah at the time. It took all the strength Leah had not to cuss this woman out for even having the nerve to dial her phone number. Leah remained calm because something inside her had already prepared her for this encounter. Leah calmly suggested that she ask her man—better yet, her fiancé—if she wanted any questions answered. Leah coolly advised the young woman to speak with her fiancé and kindly never to dial her number again.

As for her soul mate Al, he did not seem to have a soul at all or the strength to handle the situation. He did not have the courage to be honest with either one of them. Instead, Al stood in silence.

A cold chill came over Leah. She did not have the courage to feel. She instantly became numb. She had visions of herself throwing every object in the room that was not bolted down in Al's path. For a split second, she saw her hands across Al's face and around his throat. What felt like eternity in Leah's mind, were only moments in that room. Instead, Leah quickly packed her things and then left the room while Al continued to stand in silence. It would not have mattered if Al had said anything at that point. Leah had emotionally and physically checked out long before she left the room.

There was a soul tie created between Leah and Al. Despite the pain and anguish that Leah felt herself, at times she still felt sorry for Al. Something inside her believed that he did not intentionally plot to fall in love with her and then break her heart. In spite of feeling humiliated, she still loved him and could not let go even though she wanted to. If only she had waited and demanded that he wait for *sex* and *her*, as God designed.

Leah fell prey to this hunter, ultimately to her heartache. Deep down she thought he was her soul mate, her destiny, her true love. They shared a connection so deep they could feel each other even miles away. Leah was heartbroken to learn that in between their moments of connectedness despite all of the times he said, "I love you", and Al calling her his angel, he managed to propose to another woman in front of his family and friends on "Resurrection Sunday."

~

God determines who walks into your life.
It's up to you to decide who you let walk away,
who you let stay, and who you refuse to let go.

—Anonymous

~

Closing

The Man

When there is nothing left but God, that is when
you find out that God is all you need.

—Anonymous

We would both say that we are better people for learning these life lessons. All trials and tribulations are not for evil, but often God's way of strengthening you, teaching you, and/or getting you to seek him. They are, in some measure, a part of God's plan to get your attention. After years of trials and tribulations, we each began at different stages in life to truly seek God for the answers.

We each embrace the scripture from Jeremiah 29:11, For I know the plans I have for you, declares the LORD, plans to prosper you and not to harm you, plans to give you hope and a future. We encourage you to allow God to lead and direct you. We are living examples that your life will begin to change for the better. You will begin to know and understand just how much you need God in your life. You will be able to spot trouble and make better decisions. You will pay attention to the red flags and listen to your inner voice. You will be able to cope with whatever life throws your way. Trust me, you cannot do it alone or by your own strength. Develop your relationship with God; He is waiting for you to call upon Him so that He can help you. When you make the best decision of your life in becoming saved and accepting Jesus Christ as your Lord and Savior, then you receive the power of the Holy Spirit. The Holy Spirit lives inside of us and is our helper. You will experience a love that no human being can give you. You will experience a joy that this world can not give you and thank God the world cannot take it away from you. You will experience an inner peace that surpasses all understanding. There are so many people suffering daily, lost and confused from the weights of life, and the people that are in it because they do not know the creator of life. The devil came to kill, steal, and destroy; and Jesus came that you might have life and have it more abundantly. Why continue to suffer? Don't wait any longer. Seek him now! To God be the glory!

Read this prayer out loud and let God begin to lead you and give you everlasting life:

> Lord God, I admit that I am a sinner in need of salvation. I believe that Jesus died for my sins and was resurrected from the dead, is alive, and hears my prayers. Please forgive my sins and come into my life as my Lord and Savior. Fill me with your Holy Spirit. Give me a new mind, heart, and life. I invite you into my heart to help direct me in my daily decision to obey you and do your will for the rest of my life. I am taking the step to begin to live for you, Lord, and according to your word. I seek your purpose for my life and pray that no longer my will but *your* will be done. Thank you for hearing my prayer. Amen.

~

If you don't know where or how to begin to know God, start with someone you trust that knows God and ask questions. By this, I do not mean that he or she just says that they know about God, but has a life that exemplifies that God is in it. If you do not have anyone to assist you on this journey then step out on faith and attend churches in your area. You can go online and search under Churches to find a local place of worship near you or ask people around you what church they attend or if they could recommend a church. Pray and ask God, and he will lead you to the perfect church home for you. I am so excited for you as this is just the beginning and the best is yet to come!

Whispers from God

♥ Weeping may remain for a night, but rejoicing comes in the morning. (Psalm 30:5)

♥ Trust in the LORD with all your heart; and lean not on your own understanding. In all your ways acknowledge him, and he will make your path straight. (Proverbs 3:5-6)

♥ And we know that all things work together for good to those that love God (Romans 8:28)

♥ I can do everything through Him who gives me strength. (Philippians 4:13)

♥ But seek first his kingdom and his righteousness; and all these things will be given to you as well. (Matthew 6:33)

♥ Delight yourself in the LORD; and he will give you the desires of your heart. (Psalm 37:4)

♥ Your word is a lamp to my feet, and a light to my path. (Psalm 119:105)

♥ Be still, and know that I am God: I will be exalted among the nations; I will be exalted in the earth. (Psalm 46:10)

♥ God is our refuge and strength, an ever-present help in trouble. (Psalm 46:1)

♥ It is better to take refuge in the Lord than to trust in man. (Psalm 118:8)

♥ Come near to God and he will come near to you. (James 4:8)

♥ For it is with your heart that you believe and are justified, and it is with your mouth that you confess and are saved. (Romans 10:10)

♥ Therefore if anyone is in Christ, he is a new creation; the old has gone, the new has come! (2 Corinthians 5:17)

~

I asked single women, married women, and mothers alike *why* they didn't tell. Here is what some of them had to say:

~

~

- ♥ "If I told her, she would have never have left my house."

- ♥ "Some things are so extraordinary; you just have to experience it for yourself. Men, motherhood, and marriage are some of those things."

- ♥ "There is way too much to tell."

- ♥ "I thought she knew"

- ♥ "I thought about it but just never did"

- ♥ "I wanted to but…"

- ♥ "Because you didn't have a lifetime."

- ♥ "I don't know if it is an intentional decision, senility, selective memory, or just plain ole revenge why mothers do not tell their daughters about the life-changing experience of men, motherhood, and marriage."

- ♥ "Because I didn't know then and often wonder whether if I even know now."

- ♥ "Only God knows."

~

Top Ten Reading Group Discussion Questions

1. Leah and Al met in a nightclub. Do you think where and how you meet someone makes a difference? Why or why not?

2. Can you relate to the BSD factor? What experiences have you had?

3. What do you think Al was looking for in Leah that he didn't already have?

4. Can soul ties really ever be broken?

5. What do you think about courting versus dating?

6. Have you ever discovered you were in a "down low" relationship? What do you think are the warning signs to look for?

7. Do you agree that a person's relationship patterns derive from their childhood?

8. Is abuse only physical? Was Leah and Al's relationship abusive in any way?

9. What do you think about Leah's belief that love was not a choice, but rather, commitment to love was? Do you agree?

10. Now that you know, what will you do differently?

Edwards Brothers, Inc.
Thorofare, NJ USA
July 1, 2011